CRIME
SCENE

Published by Raw Dog Screaming Press
Bowie, MD
All rights reserved.
First Edition

Cover art by Don Noble

Book design: Jennifer Barnes

Printed in the United States of America
ISBN: 9781947879485

Library of Congress Control Number:
2022944245

RawDogScreaming.com

CRIME SCENE

poetry by
Cynthia Pelayo

RAW DOG
SCREAMING
PRESS

Author's Note

I never write author's notes, because I prefer for the reader to read and interpret as they will. However, in this instance, I feel it important to advise that this collection of poetry is unlike my previous collections. This is a narrative told in verse and so these poems were crafted and intended to be read in order, from report 0001 through to the final report.

Crime Scene was inspired by my Bram Stoker Award nominated poetry collection, *Into the Forest and All the Way Through*, and the readings of epic poetry. In epic poetry, we follow a hero along on their journey, tackling supernatural and human monsters, in search of something, the ultimate answer or goal. In *The Epic of Gilgamesh*, written over four thousand years ago, we learn about the hero-king Gilgamesh. After his friend Enkidu dies, Gilgamesh sets off to locate Utnapishtim, a mythical figure he believes can grant him eternal life. The quest is built upon the simple answer many of us are seeking, the meaning of life. What's also striking about *The Epic of Gilgamesh* is that we learn that Gilgamesh doesn't just fear death, but meaninglessness, and the possibility that all of this—life—holds no meaning. I will not state whether or not Gilgamesh finds his answer. Instead, I encourage you to read it.

The Epic of Gilgamesh is the oldest piece of epic poetry. By comparison, Homer's *The Iliad* and *The Odyssey* were written over 1,500 years after *The Epic of Gilgamesh*. Other epic poetry includes *Beowulf*, the *Mahābhārata*, *The Aeneid*, *The Divine Comedy*, and *Paradise Lost*. Thus, for a very long time we have been fascinated by the story of the hero who departs their home searching for answers.

So, what is an epic poem exactly, and why did I choose to write one? An epic poem is a narrative work of poetry. It is a story told through a series of poems. There are certain characteristics shared by epic poetry: third-person narration, a brave hero, a journey, supernatural elements, which often include the invocation of a muse, and the focus on a certain aspect of a culture.

Yes, *Crime Scene* is a narrative told in verse and yes, I'm calling it an epic poem. It can be both of those things. It is both of those things.

I hope that you start reading at report 0001 and follow our hero on their journey, and that's all I will say.

Everything else is open to your interpretation. I welcome that and I thank you for reading.

—Cynthia "Cina" Pelayo

Introduction
by Sara Tantlinger

"She dreams / of shimmering / dead girls" reads one of the stunning stanzas found within Cynthia Pelayo's poignant collection of narrative verse. Like much of Pelayo's other work, *Crime Scene* invites readers to enter a world where their hearts are sure to break. However, it's impossible to turn away from the pages because we fall so deep into the magic of Pelayo's words. The striking juxtapositions of life's beauty along with its nightmares are captured with spectacular clarity within the book. Here, we're invited to not only take a peek behind the caution tape, but to face murderous grief without any safety net. We are asked to become more than a spectator, and there is no turning back once the sheet is pulled down and the wrath of a cadaver demands justice.

This collection is unique in how the story is told through poetic crime reports, and the format also creates a strong urgency that perfectly matches what the characters are going through. Instantly, we're grabbed with the need to know who the suspects are, to understand why and how such terrible things can happen. We're drawn into the web with the protagonist, Agent K, and we follow along inside that sticky maze no matter what new terror traps us. The bodies being uncovered never received the opportunity to glance away from the horror that snuffed their light out, so the least we can do is follow the clues. The least we can do is witness.

From the beginning with "Report No. 0002," readers are immersed in the kind of grief that shatters a whole person into jagged slivers of who they once were. We can't look away from this story. It's one we've seen on the news, or on a trending tab on social media, and then it's gone. Here, however, Pelayo makes sure readers cannot find distraction. As a society, we've become saturated in anguish, and it's difficult to push forward, but *Crime Scene* reminds us exactly why it is so important to keep these stories alive. If we don't remember the missing and the abandoned, who will? Do we let them fade to whispers, to something like a ghost story? Not here. *Crime Scene* is not a whisper; it's a scream to remember, to demand the world become a safer and better one to live in because for so many, "there will never be another summertime lullaby" ("Report No. 0003"). Lines like this will stop readers in their tracks as they admire how much Pelayo excels at creating images and sensations that will both delight horror lovers and leave their hearts aching.

Poetry thrives on the idea of not wasting any words. Every line counts toward creating descriptions that stay with the reader; in horror poetry, those are usually haunting or visceral depictions of some kind. This method works particularly well with the subject matter of *Crime Scene* because along with each word holding importance, so does every moment that goes by for Agent K. Our hero faces the kind of darkness and torment that most of us can only imagine. Her epic journey is one that does not have a second to spare. If she isn't occupying the labyrinth in her brain with clues and evidence to solve a case, then "the mortuary of her mind," as "Report No. 0051" describes, becomes a place of unbearable torment—the kind of torment that calls out like a beacon for an audience to flock to and observe the agent as she works. Does the audience applaud, or does the audience look on in glee at the hero's suffering?

"Report No. 0012" provides a great moment where Pelayo writes, "Our hero enters stage left / Let's hold our breath as we weigh her burden to solve this." That feeling of watching Agent K, cheering her on but also knowing how quickly a group can turn into a mob. If things don't go their way, it could become just as easy to blame Agent K as it was to praise her work. These moments so seamlessly echo the voyeuristic nature of society. We are capable of uplifting someone to the highest heights, and we're just as capable of turning on them until their broken spirits are dragged down into the bleakest dregs. Agent K knows this, yet, she still carries on. The power created in these small moments by Pelayo continually show what a thoughtful, careful writer she is, and *Crime Scene* is a testament to that from beginning to end.

Along with the dark truths the collection brings, there is also a line in "Report No. 0064" that asks, "What is the hope?" It's a question I thought about a lot as I read through *Crime Scene*. How much hope can one have when they know the outcome in these particular situations won't end well? Hope is a fickle, tricky thing, yet we're desperate for it. Hungry for the chance, no matter how small, that things will get better. Given our constant access to the news, it's too easy to scroll away from headlines telling us in bold letters about the day's bloodshed. These real events start to feel like stories because there are so many of them. Too many. How do we protect our hearts without becoming completely hardened and numb? It's a difficult line to walk, but *Crime Scene* compassionately shows us the importance of remembering our humanity even in the grimmest of realities.

So let this collection invite you into the woods where butterflies and peony petals become just as haunting as missing eyelids and exposed teeth. With clever references to fairy tales and fate, this stark, beautiful ode to sorrow continues to showcase the talent Pelayo possesses as she weaves her stories. She never shies away from the brutal aspects real-life horror holds, and what is more horrifying than the violence humanity is so capable of wielding unto one another? Yet, Pelayo handles these concepts with grace, empathy, and unflinching truth, cementing *Crime Scene* as an exquisite addition to the canon of horror poetry.

—Sara Tantlinger, Bram Stoker Award-winning author of *The Devil's Dreamland: Poetry Inspired by H.H. Holmes*

To Michael—

We're here until we're not.

Report No. 0001

Crime. Confinement. Concerted. Collector. Capture. Clandestine. Clean. Court. Cancel. Courtroom. Contrast. Closet. Closure. Cigar. Counterpart. Cryptic. Covert. Compressed. Contribution. Chair. Cautionary. Client. Cigarette. Charge. Corpse. Condition. Cry. Cranium. Criminality. Confession. Complaint. Conclude. Consider. Clinical. Crepuscular. Confidence. Creative. Collect. Ceremony. Calculating. Credible. Check. Complexity. Crossing. Chamber. Conserve. Circumvent. Citation. Craftsman. Curve. Circumstance. Consume. Confirmation. Crackdown. Cracks. Confusion. Contact. Connect. Curious. Coffin. Conduct. Chaos. Crushed. Could. Chain. Corridor. Crucifixion. Cover. Conniving. Contend. Calcification. Certainly. Crash. Chance. Convey. Controversial. Cellar. Checklist. Criminology. Coffee. Clash. Confused. Clear. Capable. Character. Convincing. Concerning. Correction. Criminal. Crescent. Creation. Crude. Corrupt. Clock. Choice. Correspondent. Creep. Casualty. Chronology. Cut. Compliant. Central. Confessional. Crunch. Crimson. Cradle. Compartment. Collapse. Claustrophobia. Chief. Capital. Crying. Croon. County. Complication. Crucial. Controversy. Crashing. Cinema. Caretaker. Continue. Cement. Cellular. Credibility. Contention. Complicated. Canal. Chalk. Cooperation. Closed. Cracking. Compassion. Confidential. Curtain. Counterattack. Cutting. Consuming. Construction. Caught. Cerebral. Catching. Chase. Conflict. Compact. Chorus. Caution. Cannot. Contrary. Center. Concession. Claw. Contemplate. Circuitous. Chose. Catch. Cemetery. Contempt. Communication. Collaborate. Commiserate. Complete. Consumption. Certain. Converge. Crept. Cruelty. Constellation. Close. Conditioned. Chill. Covert. Clandestine. Castle. Cloak. Crypt. Crow. Cringe. Candy. Candles Cadaver. Casket. Clairvoyant. Conjure. Crazed. Cloak. Chills. Cough. Control. Childhood. Capacity. Chilling. Cease. Cursed.

Report No. 0002

There is screaming. *There should be screaming.* There is collapsing. There is throwing. There is crashing. There is a great tide of grief that erupts within and there's nothing to do but *wait?* Then there is wheezing, and the heavy, thick sound of mucus. There is an extension of fluids, tears, and something flowing out from pots that were on the stove just moments ago. There is trembling. There is confused communication. There is Father pressing his body against Mother and telling her...what can he tell her? There is no telling her to not feel pain, because this is glorious, all-consuming pain. This is intensity that floods synapses, that courses through and damages DNA. There is now a goal: get up from the floor. Mother cannot get up from the floor. There is now shrieking, a beg for escape, but she cannot step out of her skin. So, she moans. Sways. Accepts the stabs of a great deception. There is and will only ever be grief. There will be no forgetting. This was past. Lick the cobwebs. Step into present.

Report No. 0003

Two children's feet pedaling into forever
faster, fastest, yet, stillness finds them in movement

ripping across trails, pebbles shooting down paths
dust blooming and blossoming into clouds warning

And so, it's been foretold, in the swaying branches
within the breeze, there's hints of lavender and iron

The trees know, as do the critters that creep and crawl,
that nervous laughter will soon be captured and collected

when a bicycle meets a boulder, sending arms and legs
tumbling, scuffed knees and torn scratched elbows

The other child slows, wheels turning, eyes widening
So, what about bent and twisted metal and torn jeans?

Before them a scene will be etched into their minds
Snapshots never to be forgotten, innocence forsaken

Siblings look to the other, bidding farewell to adolescence
There will never be another summertime lullaby

"Should we call someone?" Little Brother asks Little Sister
Who is there to call? Can any adult truly fix this?

Huddled closely together they see ruin in the other,
in the phone call. The plea. "We've found a body."

Report No. 0004

Laws on electric
lines, first dial
then ring, now
beg for someone
to care, move
faster

"Yes, I am
here," and "Yes,

this is what
I see," and "No, I
will not touch
death." They are
beyond dead
"I am scared."

Inaudible crying

"Someone is on
their way." We've
all lost our way
"Hurry, my brother
is crying." *I can't.*
"Can we leave now?"
Wait
"Someone will

be there soon."
Maybe we should
not have turned
down that path
lined with bread
crumbs soaked
in blood, and is
that a howl I hear?
It smells of gingerbread
Maybe we were lured
here, to our own
destruction

"I see
the flashing lights."

Report No. 0005

Little Brother pleads to leave
"We can ride away into forever"
Words mean nothing
Death, an uninvited burden
Motion already at play

Sensory traps settling
Brains registering environment
Auditory cues: gasps in throats
Choked-back screams
Spectacular relic on display

"Maybe it's fake?" Little Sister says
kicking the remains of something that once was
Little Brother turns, a disoriented dance
His body collapses beneath him
Blackened bones glisten in his vomit

Brother pleads, there's no obeying these
discordant and dissonant bird songs

"We should've gone left," Little Brother says

"There's no left and nothing's right."
"This is our forever," Little Sister says

Beating blue and red lights approach

The mourning call is captured

Little Brother weeps.

Little Sister stands, and says:
"She's been dead a long time."

Report No. 0006

Operator:	911. What is your emergency?
Little Sister:	It looks like a perfectly positioned porcelain doll
Operator:	911. What is your emergency?
Little Sister:	The leaves, golden brown, red, and green, a forest blanket
Operator:	911. What is your emergency?
Little Sister:	I think I hear her breathing. Can skeletons breathe? I see her rib cage rise and fall, gently. Maybe because it's windy here, caused by the beating wings of beasts, fireflies, or is it a butterfly?
Operator:	911. What is your emergency?
Little Sister:	Is that what we all look like when we die? Will we die? Did we die? I know I died today, but how will I explain that to Mother?
Operator:	911. What is your emergency?
Little Sister:	My brother is crying. You can ignore him. He does not know all of the things that I know, and he will need to remember to make it to the end of this story.
Operator:	911. What is your emergency?
Little Sister:	I wonder, do you know all of the things about me? I hope not, for I have a secret.

20

Operator:	911. What is your emergency?
Little Sister:	As I fall asleep, I lay very still, a corpse on cold, pink sheets. Will my death be televised, streamed across platforms, and discussed by those interested in profit over justice?
Operator:	911. What is your emergency?
LittleSister:	My dreams are blood and sinew and fatty tissue, and it's sticky sweet.
Operator:	911. What is your emergency?
Little Sister:	Maybe I was never a child. Maybe I'm tendons and ligaments wrapped in gauze. Maybe this is all something else and none of this matters?
Operator:	911. What is your emergency?
Little Sister:	Perhaps I like what I see.
Operator:	The police are on their way.
Little Sister:	I know, but it doesn't really matter.

Report No. 0007

Her cellphone rings
and she begs the fates
for a silent night

but this will not be normal
Electronic song signals fury,
the end of normality.

Why resist?

The three of them listen
Atropos, Lachesis, Clotho
Thread, spinning life and death

Do we each have a destiny?
Agent K doesn't believe so
There's life, death, sometimes murder

She accepts she'll go forward
towards her own oblivion, this task
a beginning she directs towards her own undoing

Report No. 0008

She rises from bed and notices a crack in her window
fingerprints, fingertips, a nightstand of murder mysteries
dust jackets with stamped skulls stacked on her bed

It's enticing to sleep with a head full of ghosts not hers
to shake away dreams of splayed and sprawled bodies
glistening throats and coagulated blood under spotlights

She draws her knees up and opens her mouth to call out to
anyone, but they come and go, nauseous from noxious smells
gun smoke, red brick, decay, cobwebbed moldy basements

Tortured, she blinks back what she's seen between miniblinds
numb from unsympathetic confessions like "I split her in two."
They savor each tear spilled on floorboards and packed dirt

A white bird crashes into her window, yesterday it was a cardinal
They want to escape the outside, crawl into her locked rooms
The phone rings again, and it might as well be laughter

She will tell them what she dreams: locks of hair, cigarette butts
a nail file, a worry doll, a glass eye meandering, a vial of pills
camera focused, black leather gloves gripping tight, long hair

Allow a drop of blood to fall onto the altar at midnight, mistaken
hunches or prophecy, and it's all a guess, a person's gaze
patternless wandering, erratic movements, she knows shadows

Report No. 0009

The call came and went, an apparition
at her footsteps, seamless instruction

Drive to this place, park there, and walk
a winding path, past a creek and listen

There will be a circus of useless people
yellow tape and flashing bulbs

A perfect task for a Sunday afternoon, find her,
look at her, tell us what happened to her

Much of the discovery was luck, after all
What is luck, but a ripple, a fluke, a glitch?

Impossibility, improbability made possible
Blessed with notions of a sacrifice, a patron deity

She once carved the number seven into her palms
Scars healed over pink made her a prophet somehow

Ravens nest in her attic, black cats sleep on her porch
At night, an owl lulls her to sleep, perched atop a pine

Every mirror in her house has cracks she cannot explain
Salt tumbles from shakers, all markers of superstition ignored

Still, the number thirteen has followed her this life
Thirteen murders, cold, staring out at her from glass coffins

Crime Scene

Report No. 0010

What did you see?
Was there someone
here with you?
Lurking, leering

gnawing at bits
of desiccated flesh
when you arrived?
The children whisper

Stunned, parents besieged
covering heads to escape
unknown detrimental downfall
How do we escape this?

One is eight, the other
nine, lives disrupted
when they discovered daisies
sprouting from eye sockets

In the car, Mother presses
Little Sister. "What did you see?"
Father's demands are rage
"Little Brother, what did you hear?"

Little Sister will refuse to disclose
the figure hiding behind
bare branches who waved hello

Report No. 0011

We trust the universe and what does it hand us? A child's corpse
people milling about, apologies through weak observations
they stand in their stiff-faced seriousness feigning concern

Other emotions squirm; curiosity for our morbid
disgust for those overwhelmed with a growing list of signatures
turning, there is always turning, an archived roster of names
a telephone wire cut, a single well-worn shoe out of place
Perhaps ask yourself as you watch them, watching time wasted

standing, talking, laughing, yes, there is laughing, not open
it bubbles within their eyes, it's joyous for them, another one
to do what? What do they do? They walk in circles and stare
Vultures waiting to peck and tear at the rotted flesh that remains

Perhaps this is why we keep the public away, not to maintain
sanctity, not to preserve fibers and hairs, but to prevent them
from seeing the empty motivations who are eager to entomb
to allow her parents to revisit and regret. Is retirement here yet?

Report No. 0012

Here comes our agent, down the hiking path lined with riddles
She wavers, like a hallucination, searching, always searching
Calculating each step, hands at her sides, eyes photographing

Balance: she hears them. They exhale, useless caretakers relieved
for the arrival of our protagonist. Our hero enters stage left
Let's hold our breath as we weigh her burden to solve this

Badges aglint in the sinking sunlight, no warrant
needed, there are shouts, and flickers, and rearranging
A warning tears apart. "Agent K," she is ordered

"This first look could destroy you," Agent M warns
Agent K shakes her head. They do not know her fractures
"I'm already broken," she says, feeling fissures widening within

Agent K sees people walk and part, a movie scene on repeat
A fellow agent's clenched jaw reminds her of her split molar
The medical examiner stands from his crouched position

The first officer on scene closes his notebook, his face grim
She thinks, they all believe themselves experts here, don't they?
Gather around, as Agent K makes her initial observations

Caretaker to the dead, perhaps secondhand participant to murder
Is this her sole task? No, this is a Rubik's Cube,
a puzzle of a thousand possibilities of how this came to be

Now enter the labyrinth, Agent K, and locate the minotaur

Report No. 0013

Cameras lowered. Agent K wonders: *Did she really exist?*
Experts step back and away. She loosens the crime scene tape,
Yellow and black, death, carefully gift wrapped, for her, always

Agent K knows this image will be terrible, we live to avoid death
We should not merely stand by and observe, stand in this circle
meditate on this fervent anxiety, exist in this fantastic nightmare

No body, no case, but here we certainly have a complete incident
Is there identification belonging to the decayed? Silence. Hum.
Followed by gestures and roles, pointless opposing discourses

Some days she tires over how prescriptive this all feels, sterilized
There's only ever two ways this will end, failure or . . .
Procedures are often misaligned, an expectation to extrapolate

Slide a glove over a hand to understand what happened before
There is a pause, a memory, a half-light in a sunken corridor
Analyze the movements, she pleads with herself, the door shuts

Image dissolves into words that do not match what unfolded
Let's try to maintain that this is not fiction, turn down lonely
roads, trajectory, this will take moments, years, a lifetime

Report No. 0014

As they speak, she'll engage
conversation, not with them
with our unnamed, considering
colors and textures, positioning

Agent K asks for the children
who were sped away by parents
shaken by the little one's fears
Little Sister smiled. Little Brother cried.

For some there is pleasure in tragedy
Agent K was that little girl, once
Her ever trusting best friend, Sage
entered a black car, and never returned

It was a day like today, they all are, wrapped
in kindness and care, but as hours tick
a scythe appears, splintering expectations
There will be no safety here or anywhere

Flashbacks pierce a veil, and she hears
mothers beg for the return of children
who will never appear, expectations
smashed of any purpose to resolve

Tight within a skeletal grasp. A beautiful clue
Talking ceases, cameras click, a voice states
confusion, but our Agent K knows too well
"Freshly wrapped sage bundle," she informs

Report No. 0015

Here is what happens at the Medical Examiner's Office.

There is no identifiable source of light.
Agent K holds a hand to a shadow on a green-tiled wall
Child, children, a true story is evolving, a canvas submerged
Could there be a relation? She wonders, but now is not the time
Wanted. Black car. Wanted. Man or woman. Person. Wanted.

Now is not the time.

"Agent K," Agent M whispers. "Start at the beginning."
He shouldn't be gentle. He shouldn't be calm. He shouldn't be.
"There was a stage. A light. A textbook. A fetus. Hands. Frame."
I already suspect, and no words escape, but her lips move
Mother inhabits her heart, this is why she cannot feel any longer

Breathe. Leaning. Louder.

"What do you want to say?" Agent K's calmness is supernatural.
"There is a future," she begins, and she knows she is not in it
"We weren't children before, nor beautiful, and we fell and I failed." "Begin
everywhere then," Agent M says. Agent K is trying to locate that place that
seizes, she begins observations:

"Disemboweled. Dismembered. Hand pulled back. Rib cage split. Equal
parts. Coagulation. A kind of orchestra. A grand chorus. Systemic erasure.
A blurring. A landscape painting. Swollen. Bleeding. Contusions. Fractures.

Missing pieces. Dried flecks of blood like shimmering stars sweep across a face asleep in infinite."

There is more and she continues, and they listen and they nod and when it's all over Agent M tells her she did a great job, and what is so great about communion with the dead? There's nothing, *great*. Only she is meant to understand, acquiring the perfect belief, the simplest symptom. This all holds resonance.

With, through her.

Report No. 0016

A labyrinth beckons
Enter, be consumed
Stretched, emerald hedges

Who trims this maze?
Jewel floating in Crete
No, dead ends branching

Interlinked, dark depths within
Ovid tells of the great Daedalus
who built a fortress to conceal a beast

Directed by the Oracle of Delphi
Shun the monster birthed by lady
Nourished by human flesh

"Part man and part bull"
He lurks in the shadows, waiting
Hunted around corners

Only a hero can solve
an endless puzzle
stretched into forever

Where lies the real victory?
Destroy the Minotaur
Escape the pattern

Crime Scene

Report No. 0017

Guide and guardian of souls
I'll mediate your conscious
unconscious, realms

Birds fluttering
Rabid dogs pacing, Cerberus
identify your creature

Charon, chart your course
an afterlife misplaced
rivers still, untouched

I will wait for the dying
I will do so myself
it's been me for eternity

pathetic and frightened
ferrywoman charged with
ushering your corpses

your decay motivates me
your final words excite me
your life's fragments bring me ecstasy

and I yearn to experience your suffering
instead, I'm damned with rearranging
the shattered pieces of you

Report No. 0018

An unjust death
taken, tortured
mocked in misery

hopeless against a backdrop
of blue sky, wondering
when will this pain end?

You are an unfinished portrait
painted most painfully
canvass punctured by cries

Heaven, what celestial
beings could exist and watch
clothes ripped, wrists wrapped

there are some who speak of
vengeful spirits, the energetic
remains of a life taken forcefully

death followed by grueling despair
body disposed of unceremoniously
disintegrating at the altar of depravity

I do not speak the words of legends or myth
I do not sing the gospel of demons, saints, or gods
I am a restless spirit in disguise

guided by a longing to bury you in earth
where clovers will spring and water
will erupt at points of those taken

Report No. 0019

Agent K is in demand
"You need something from me?"

Unspooled VHS tape ribbons
Grand affair, expose the investigator

"You already have everything you need.
What is it that you require from me?"

People beg her to save them from death
slipped into an abandoned well

crippling singed, oily memories
stars extinguished burned black

What is draped across an old chair?
A matchstick, sewing needle, thread

Houses drifting, neighborhoods fading
Framed pictures of shattered moments

No one recalls moments before the last We know the past was written as
deceit

Frozen in phones lines, underdeveloped pictures
Faded negatives curled in shoeboxes, tossed

Secondhand stores, incinerated, burnt ephemera
Light hope spilling through stained glass

Here we are sick, a different sort of disease
A symptom that crowds, detonates

Prick me, I want to wake you in the morning
You can start again fresh as a new resurrection

Dew drops on the tip of my tongue,
I'd rather feel pressed metal, a warm flow

Hand me the blade and slowly press it into my neck
Feel the tension tighten, swallowing back all you know

Report No. 0020

External, internal examination
pathologist removes, dissects
completely still, precision

opens chest, expose abdominal
pelvic organs, with all of this
comes little blood, no pressure

only a beating heart produces
streams, gravity dysfunction
here: hands, legs, arms, a face

body arched beneath blocks
a torso dully exposed, Y-shaped
incision, to slip off and slip on

curved beneath breasts
freed intestines
cut down the crown

spongy brain cradled
floating in formalin
tissue and gray matter

lists abnormalities, unusual
liquids pour into bags and vials
blood, urine, vitreous eye gel

Your organs paint a portrait
leaked across tests like a
great abstract landscape

Report No. 0021

Marks left behind
smudges, smeared
oil along edges

swirled impressions
lines, scattered
randomized

deliberately pressed
surfaces marked as
smooth, inconclusive

mirrors, wood, plastic
natural materials
inconsequential

raised epidermis
your biology makes
its case against you

Spot the arch, loop
winding whorls
Are they even there?

Single finger or
entire hands spread
against radial loops

exemplar, palm
scanned detect
make clearer
naked eye, or
pull in details
angles, position

calculate space
visible, patent
print

Moisture betrays
you, porous
nonporous

A single fingerprint
lifted, identify the
corpse, find the

culprit

Report No. 0022

She dreams
of shimmering
dead girls
pools of them

Cupid's lips
baby's breath
mother's milk
crow's feet

What is left behind
a shoe, a slip,
bra strap, cell phone,
shiny new lip gloss

At night they awake
serve her delicious
secrets of what was
done, most barbarically

In the morning they wake
her with crystalized tears
hot summer wind, howling
winter breeze, raindrops

Dew and melt, curled
at feet, prep and spin

a tale most vile, how
to resist it as it repeats

Agent K brushes
their hair, she wipes
their cheeks, dabs
eyes, morning drives

Across the city, scanning
tombstones, headstones,
clearing away dust, years
where she'll cradle her dead

She'll dig through
dirt, open
caskets, pull at
rusted hardware

to set them free
they're fluttering
within coffins
plucked butterflies

waiting to be
reborn only to die
again

Report No. 0023

In a crowd of people
everyone looks the same,
there's sneers and teeth,

rabid breath
crinkling, noses,
fangs waiting to sink

She wonders

which ones will bite,
because they all can

Dig sharp teeth
in the meat of necks
pulling away skin

fat and tendons
dancing with glee
an artery sprays

a fire hydrant
cracked open
on a boiling day

They all want
a piece of her

catered regrets

an heirloom
to regurgitate
all of her failures

all of the bloated
blue bodies
pictures that line

her walls
reminding her
always forcing her

to bow beneath
the failure she was
is,

has been
will forever be
she cannot save them

she cannot protect them
they will beg
they will die

their cries will replay
within walls and forests
forming new sounds

freshly birthed
cardinals, their fluffy
red feathers

a red streak against
the sky, but it's all
lies masked as surrender

for another case sits beneath broken florescent lights

Report No. 0024

One learns
to live with
their thoughts

a slow-moving corpse
it's better to
listen, realize

the full extent
of fear's approach
understand, deep

within jumbled
disjointed, decayed
jagged movements

offer no sympathy
resign to it
relish in it

the ecstasy of dread
terror as orgasm

Report No. 0025

Days pass in mass
a wave, a sigh, hush
gray-streaked sky

let's start with a belief
face void of expression
afraid to be seen

Let's draw him, take
stabs, guessing
impatient, unbearable

Did they line pages with
knives as bookmarks?
Does the story end there?

Rip off the cover lest
it vanishes without
careful determination

Relics of a mood
which exists in a moment
cradle like glowworms

Press your palm against
its body to emit light
attract but never defend

Is that why you took
a bite of her? You're
made of bitter poison

Report No. 0026

Let's start at the beginning, Agent K says
She closes the window, perhaps to trap the truth within
His eyes dart. "Have you been sleeping?" Agent M asks.
"Sleep offers no clarity or salvation," Agent K responds.

It's a language aiming for precision, missing expectation
Misunderstandings evolve into great production
Words are hidden, within the crevices, sunken caverns
"See what I mean?" she says. "Write what we know."

Dates. Names. Receipts. Wake up time. Start and stop.
Recount everything you know and have ever known.
Feel the great weight of the world between us. Speak with
suspect. You knew her, once. She loved you, once.

"Why are you afraid to utter her name right now?"
Pen to paper, move faster, "No need to stir restless spirits."
Mental note: Detachment. Cold. Complacent. Unsympathetic
A stillness that mocks, utters contempt for motions and gravity

A long silence as they stare down, predator prey, pray, prays
Or, villain, antagonist, who finds bliss in the blooming lie
Needle and thread and stitch words onto maps, push thumbtacks
Note suspect's body language as they utter: woods, body, before

"It isn't me," our suspect says.
Agent K demands for the forest to be upended and understood

"I need an explanation of each split branch and crunched leaf."
Our first suspect looks across to the knowing mirror:

"This is an imaginary room."

Report No. 0027

Suspect 1 dies before we could speak again
Agent K plays back his voice
"I cannot trust anyone," Suspect 1 said.
She measures the breaks as her own

"I am trying to gather slips of truth."
Her words beg for a path forward
"What is this worth to you?" Suspect 1 asked.
Silence. Revelation. Absolution.

"We will need to speak again," she said.
"I did not say a word," he fades.
Therein lies the problem
"Figure this out for yourself!"

In that moment he knew what he'd do
A chair. A rope. A cigarette in an ashtray.
Agent K later agrees: "It wasn't him."
He had other warrants. Other stories.

With his life highlighted beneath a microscope
panic settled. A flailing sea creature sinking
beneath an unforgiving sea as she learned
his name, discovered what he'd hidden

there were accusations of fraud, money
filtering down pipes away from those who

required it. Stories of people silenced
cars that veered off roads mysteriously

"An innocent man killed himself," Agent M says.
"No one is ever truly righteous," Agent K offers.
We all have secrets, not all of us is a murderer, but
none of us are innocent of any and all accusations

"We have his alibi," Agent K stresses.
He is cleared of this case, but not of his wrongs
Awaiting her thoughts, she will
not measure or speak of the injustice of this all

We are all guilty of our crimes and we will all
pay within time, facing our true selves for each
of our blistering failures. For now, we remain in
service, continuing to search for our killer

Report No. 0028

What have you been presented with?
Are you following along with logic,
reason, or falling down depths of fallacy?

Who is the killer? Do you have a clue?
Facts, a hunch, an intuition, a deep
suspicion that validates your conclusion

Do you know? Do you think you know?
Or are you allowing yourself to be led here?
Follow us down this glittering gallery

Take inventory of what you have been provided
What are you missing? Are you ill-equipped
To make a determination?

Nothing is as it seems, like Alice tumbling down
into madness and revelry, a cast of spectacular
characters who are all suspect

Divert, do not make a conclusion yet
or you shall be wrong, these literary devices
smell of smoked fish

Are you purposefully being led astray?
Perhaps. This is our rhetorical strategy
Examine. Prod. Poke. Point. Press.

A grand conclusion takes twists and turns
An "Aha!" An "I knew all along." But, did you?
Sit back and be distracted by the play unfolding

It's close. It's swimming in your periphery
A red herring

Report No. 0029

Some return
a visit in
tribute

or, something
fluttering in
the grave

revisiting
replaying
rewinding

lusting over
unholy results
feeling time

repeating
ravishing, a
rapture

movie screen
of the mind
screams pulse

ghost reliving
echoes, unable
to rest

Report No. 0030

From one he clipped a lock of hair
summer wheat harvested the night
of the strawberry moon

Another clutched tightly to a pack
of chewing gum, as if that could
save her, he laminated the wrapper

A third liked to read his tarot cards
she wiped her brow when the Devil
appeared, it lives in his wallet now

From others there are baubles, gold
chains and stopped watches
class, engagement, wedding rings

He caresses silk scarves at night, the
scent faded, pens, mascara, a retainer
business cards, a plane's boarding pass

Car keys and bus tickets sit in a bowl beside
the door, there's relief knowing they can't
be used to whisk his beauties away

Several pair of earrings, strung delicately
like Christmas garland. He takes joy in
the shadows they cast, happiness and horror

trapped in his house

Cynthia Pelayo

Report No. 0031

At night she speaks to the dead
wandering her apartment, listing
a recitation of names, birthdates
stars, celestial bodies flooding
above, below, gravity is useless

or evolving, erupting, new phase all
within an incongruent expectation
she marks signatures thumbtacked
to a great wall connecting, never

relating, to accounts soldered

It's interlaced, woven, somehow
the stars must meet at some level
of order, one rotates, one is fixed
another comet bursts across the sky
still, we do not know the impulse

If moon affects the tide, then how
can a human made from flesh
unravel all the broken trophies
Name. Sky. Movement. Motive.
Expansive and worthless constellations

She continues to pace as sun rises
moon sets, the Earth continues

its dire direction, offering little
hope, always moving, twisting
come around the flow of disaster

Report No. 0032

At night there's always tapping
disembodied against a window
pain. Doorknob rattles, ghosts
pleading to be allowed in, speak

Tonight, Agent K sleeps
breaking free from the expectation
to understand and to save
even though slumber offers little rest
Noises reach into her dreams
titanium claws dipped in acid
she awakes, shaking remnants of
a life in which she loved and was loved

Snowflakes float across her bed
windows and doors open, night
ushers in a waring, funeral bell
winter wind carries whispers

Sitting up she shakes the sands
of a dream and sees what is outside
is in. Doors. Windows. Unlocked.
A blizzard erupts around her.

Someone was in her house

Report No. 0033

What did you see?
an old wound

There's a phrase
as if, I don't know

Suggest the truth
mutate the story

Over time, stiches
wandering, halves

End day. Scraps
garish color

Screams pecking
at one another

Crumpled cans
balled up paper

We teeter on an
explanation, or excuse

She's asked things
doors and windows

Locks and latches
irresponsibility

Surely, it must be
her fault, she's tired

One murmurs, another
laughs, upsetting

It's all underwater
light, forms pushed

Distorted faces, all
blurred predators

Their flesh plucked
pulled from fat

What do you think?
What do you want?

She wants to believe
no one was within

She wants answers
pinned to hearts

Letters, dates, names
hacked out from

Violation, who
watched her

as she slept?

Crime Scene

Report No. 0034

I'd like to invite
the reader to solve
this for Agent K

Take a step back
or peer into a box
see gun pressed

temple, skull
resting on silk
music appears

a room of long
faded memories
blood soaks and
covers every
surface, all
remain, invisible

if you smell rot
you are close
now try, pause

something awful
is happening
the killer is trying

to get rid of a
witness
our blood whispers

a knife sharpened
impressions emergegloves, plastic sheeting

Breathe quietly now

Report No. 0035

Shred flesh
larynx cut

fingernails
removed

rope, lots of
rope, knotted

thin places
bloody blade

uncontrollable
events, hidden

torn dress, a
shoe, missing

Cinderella's
slipper

no one knows
the full story

The shot came
from behind

as she dangled
bullet casings

another afternoon
brand new murder

Why did the killer
return?

It's still too early
to tell

Crime Scene

Report No. 0036

Agent K cannot afford
doubt, worry, a wrong
must be righted, clearly

Distinct opposites, polar
good and evil, a paradox
tucked between twilight

Be meticulous. Do not lose.
sight. Laborious observing.
Checking and rechecking

She insists that she is fine
untouched by the weight
untangling mangled corpses

Memory holds on streaks
of tear-stained blue cheeks
hair matted with dry vomit

"I am fine," she repeats only
to herself, unconvinced by
fragments of cadavers

The dead eclipse the living
bloody edges holding us in
place, at night the wind blows

withered leaves
across her bedsheets

Cynthia Pelayo

Report No. 0037

Let's inspect
the action

sudden and
searching

body pulled
back savagely

who decides
who lives

flashes of
blue and red

twinkling across
treetops

we are insane
to seek truth

we are the story
ceaseless to depart

when she visits
the new scene

stones outline the
shape of our girl

Report No. 0038

An envelope arrives
Addressed to Agent K
Signed: "Your admirer"

No one admires our
Agent, no one longs
for bloodstained nightmares

Failures etched within her
skin, peeling back captured
screams of families betrayed

World without reason, chaos
gnawing on the flesh of
fawns as they squirm

There is no admiration in
failed duty to something
that cannot be controlled

Murder. Vengeance. Revenge.
Lunacy. Disregard for humanity.
Annihilating innocence with glee

For she knows that in order to
understand a monster, she must
embrace the transformation herself

There is coldness, neglect
failed saints are condemned
for inadequacy, corruption

A system that plays into
destruction of communities
is a vulture embodied

Picking and pecking apart
she cannot deny this
will continue as she ends

Crime Scene

Report No. 0039

At night she hunts
darkness, unscrewing
lightbulbs smearing
liquid black mascara
across eyelids, hoping
paint darkened light
perhaps then she could
see. Tucked in corners
women with stories
bodies dismantled,
obliterated beneath
frenzied hands, tying
only those of her kind
can process, weight
damnation of knowing
what a body looks like
frozen forever, seized
fists clenched, clasped
eyes peering into oblivion
unable to connect or
keep a promise in belief
of a corrupted heaven
nothing is willing to save
you as you die alone
Agent K was assigned
to speak with someone
find cures within comfort

instead, she
stands in front of a mirror
lips tight on her reflection
experiencing every bruise
seen waiting for welts to
emerge in networks
vibrant nightmares
dancing in her brain
her doppelgänger nods
shadow selves know
discomfort, apologies
unhooking from her
own movements
"What now?" Our
Agent K asks questions

The mirrored form
laughs from within
eyes still, expression lost
no words to discover
flesh trapped in form
what wonders could her
devil divulge?

Report No. 0040

Putrefaction spread its grip
a performance scheduled
for our investigator, process

viewed in three acts, by
a loathsome hiking trail
an audience of maggots
feasted on misery, murder

Fluids seeped, a body cried
nothing is normal, witnessing
beauty succumb to wasting

Her skin glows in postmortem
stain. Deep purple, shimmering
reds. Livor mortis. Hours passed.

Muscles grew rigid. Rig-or. Algor.
Perfume so distinct from bloat
putrescine with hints of cadaverine

Skin loosened against muscle
as if this is all a costume,
a ball where no invite
was requested

Eyes bulge pleading, swollen
tongue trapped in a mouth that
last knew screams

Cynthia Pelayo   73

Report No. 0041

Tragedy is able to loosen us from routine
We feel pinpricks succumbing to destruction

We are offerings to those wielding knives
Slicing through skin, hacking fine cartilage

Glistening bones scattered across ground
Surrounded by beauty, nestled in cement

I want to taste your final tears, moaning
in your ear that I will find you, believe me

No one seems to accept I've regarded
sympathy as the symphony for murder

Report No. 0042

We have two bodies now
A girl and a woman
What separates either?

Age

Expanse of time
milestones, tides
possibility and a vow

My dear

Verily sacred promise
carefully treasured
pearl plucked from seashell

Unprotected

Grown with love
within seconds end
trapped in a rusted cage

Dripping

With a substance sticky sweet
between trembling fingers
cracked and broken nails

Defiance

Once delightfully sparkling
gem of a human
crudely held up to harsh

Light

To be analyzed and inspected
whose painted butterfly wings
were pinned

Mounted

Not on a board
not with delicate care
instead with precision

Brutality

Hold me, caress me, gently in your memory

Report No. 0043

New, Suspect 2
Older than last
Presents receipts
Devasted in their
Consideration

"I was nowhere
near" Agent K
verifies each slip
phone calls, cameras
it's never enough

Our new suspect
collapses in grief
being shown photos
of a dislocated person
human puzzle pieces

"Where is the rest of
her?" Our suspect asks
"In a park? Car? Between
floors? A cold pillowcase?"
Agent K questions
Vomit splashes against
metal tabletop, black
liquid smelling of sulfur
anxiety. "I was nowhere

near..." No longer a suspect

Exit stage left

Another failure, lost grasp
mind races past names
dates, photographs, prints
Someone missed, cleared
She'll start again at zero

Report No. 0044

Sometimes Agent K wonders if he ever thinks of her
rejected for her decision to marry the murdered, instead
on the new moon she plays back a voicemail she saved
just to hear him say her name one last time, the sound staticky

Lingering on a single letter, and instead of her name it sounds
like *Kill*. Accepting your fate is often worse than dying
We all reach a point where our plot has been written, her name
rearranged, she accepted the capitalized note, Agent K

It could have been her lover in bed next to her. Yet, in his place
a pillow pinned with crime scene photos, her brilliant girls
dead and rotting. They can never leave her. She handles
their memory delicately, like antique lace, vintage stained glass

Report No. 0045

This is how she lost her –

They were friends, neighbors,
Years past, the two inseparable:
Birthdays, lip gloss, new hairstyles
Trading secrets on bedroom floors
Her name rests on K's tongue eternal

Together they walked to the bus
Together they entered school
Together they floated down hallways
Together they departed from another

"They say they'll give us a ride."
Four pair of sunken eyes peered back
"Where will we sit," K asked?
"We'll squeeze in," fault of innocence
Sage was a blistering noon day sun fading

Agent K still feels those lips
And the departing sting of "I'll be fine."
Agent K still remembers ringing
Telephones, strangers knocking
Answering, unspooling questions, the cries

"How could you allow her to get in?
that car? Those strangers? How?"

Abandoned? Next door, there's
sounds of
wailing, an animal dying. Days.
Weeks. Months. Decades. Bundled.

In irreparable agony tasting of regret.

Report No. 0046

Her ghost stalks Agent K
murmuring at the foot of her bed
seated at the breakfast table
always there, but never in reach

time taunts us with wondering
creates memories of moments
never materialized, laughter that
remains unprocessed in mouths

Instead, there are two ghosts:
Agent K and her great failure.
Sage wants to wake our Agent
And demand:

You did not kill me

Those bruises on my thighs
Clotted blood swallowed; hair torn
from raw scalp, none of it was you
Believe in my final moments

All I thought of was you
No one will ever believe
I did not want this for you
Know that I fought death

As Agent K awakens to a new day
she ignores the ghostly impression on her bed
brushes away a kitchen chair moved an inch
remaining unable to hear a call from beyond

Report No. 0047

Method of murder
Means of detecting
All that you know

The truth? Total

Immersed and clear
What blinds us
Leading to a surprise

Never speak of "feelings"
Detach from yourself
Purposed only to calculate

Solve

Report No. 0048

Agent K knows we are the monsters
Gnarled teeth and sharpened talons
Ready to strike and gnaw, splintering

We destroy and consume what we lust
Sinking our teeth in raw fear, relishing screams
Consumed by bliss while intensifying the attack

Agent K has learned the way of deviance
Attuning to the vibration of evil, to understand
Walking down dark corridors, smelling smoke

Joining together in what can destroy her in order
To understand, shards of broken bone brush past
Her cheeks, slice into her skin, but she accepts

The ashes of innocent ignorance, makes a trade
For blood-soaked bathrooms, hints of bleach, hair
Forced down clogs, shattered teeth, muddy footprints

We're all the same within, but some of us just want
to rip insides out, scatter intestines across floors picking
out the pleasures to read the (mis)fortunes in our futures

Report No. 0049

"Where were you?" Agent Masks our dear Agent K

she cannot tell him
she packed a bag last night

drove to the trail and spread
a blanket over the very spot

they found our girl outstretched,
her arms and legs, a corpse angel.

hoping to sense what our dead sensed
hoping to see what our dead saw
she closed her eyes and heard
an owl screech overhead

finding comfort in night creatures
accepting her own vulnerabilities

The fate that we all will die like this,
alone. She finally slept that night.

Report No. 0050

It's far too early to accept
she'll wake in the morning
to a sky people will
be born beneath, a day when
lovers' faces will be caressed

it's far too early to accept
not everyone knows what
rotting and blackened skin
peeled-back brittle fingernails
textures beneath rubber gloves

it's far too early to accept
normality gives us false joy
living, existing, unscarred by
grief guiding us all, useless star

a point of access into oblivion

Report No. 0051

At home she covers her floor in newspaper clippings
Black, white, and red confetti, **THE LATEST VICTIM**
Headlines taunt, excite, people like to be teased with grief
so long as it's not their own personal pain to experience

Scraps of notebook paper cover her desk, photographs
napkins from coffee shops she's visited across the city
some covered in names, dates, numbers of people she's
met but refused to allow into the mortuary of her mind

No one should suffer needlessly, and so she'll carry
reports. Quotes. Statements. Files. Records. Memorize,
Not just *memorize*, but *know*, recall, string pieces together
What are the logistics? What are the beating hearts of this story?

We all conjured miracles into existence by a series of
unrelated events. *I can't figure this out!* She slams a hand down.
She is the trope. Martyr. Tortured. She will wear this
character until she wastes and decays in her silk-lined coffin

Report No. 0052

Shock is crystalline pure
Every case, and perhaps
We should not call them
Case. Perhaps give us a name.
An instant of shock and then pity
We wish to admit our horror
But we relish in the exquisite details
We long to feed off their suffering
Tragedy with our coffee
The kidnapped with our lunch
For dinner we consume snuff films
Passed off as documentaries
Agent K admits excitement
Creeps when there's a call
Approaching it as a challenge
Newfound opportunity assembled

Is any of this unfolding fast
enough for you? Do threads
of thrill, curiosity grow within
you bearing witness to death?

Report No. 0053

Witness presented
Relax, take comfort
Show me what you
Saw

I see her, C turns
crossing the street
tosses crumpled
paper in a trashcan

C waits, sees me
gaze past a mirage
intended to penetrate
there's a revision

Her skin seems to
part, organs presented
as apparatus. She is a
velvet curtain unfurling

Now we're on stage,
while C is our audience
offering a standing ovation
for our mismanagement

Agent K nods, considering
the notepad just a repetition of words wounded with worry
"This is all an endless fog"

Our witness rises, repeats
"That day I saw C in those clothes
crossing that street
entering that trail. That's all."

Report No. 0054

Coroner's report for the second victim, C

The corpse was discovered in a preliminary state of decay. Corpse, noted as C herein is a woman of a certain age, of a
certain body type, of a certain hair color, of a certain eye color,
of a certain race, of a certain ethnicity, from a previous certain background noted as: human — once alive. Current state: No longer alive. Key findings include: Dried blood, matted hair, missing fingernails, eyelids removed in their place, butterfly wings, painted ladies. Teeth are intact, gleaming, ears however remain missing, in their place, pink peony petals.

Report No. 0055

Agent K stays up tonight
waiting for the murderer to call
expecting to be taunted, tormented
it wasn't an accident, another note
left, this one telling her
how much he enjoyed watching
her movements in the morning
walking across the parking lot
balancing keys and phone, a
backpack with the letter K
stitched into the fabric. The
perpetrator asks "Are you no longer
Karma, going simply by K as
if you've misplaced the meaning
of your actions in your prior life?"
If he expects her to cry her tears
are reserved for fresh burial plots
"Did you know K, that a crafted
torso can be made to stay alive…"
She imagines him smiling here,
the ink drives deep into the fibers of the paper there, automatic writing
a love letter from our murderer enjoying her aching d
iscomfort
there's ringing in her ear'Where?' is all she cares to know,
Where is her Sage? Where are
the others? Bones scattered
dark gloves, these are the tokens

that wreck her, and now
pages, these letters, and the
pleasure our killer gains only
extends Agent K's purgatory

Report No. 0056

The DNA results return
coils, human coordinates
genetic measurements

calculations, can numbers
dictate to us what happened
replaying scenes

arithmetic cannot explain
computed barbarity inflicted
it's only a test of markers

We know she was a child
aged 14 to 18, further exams
indicate killer returned

again, removing pieces
of delicate vertebrae
here, readjusting positions

fingerbones there, jaw
angled where? With her
he has taken great care

Perhaps he enjoys that
Agent K is so close
still, he remains undetected

Report No. 0057

Someone turns themselves in
claiming to be the murderer
when asked of their intentions
they speak of ends, civilization
perched high upon a pulpit
lizards and snakes wrapped
around scripture smelling of
frankincense and we are
failures as progress. They closetheir eyes and hum a lullaby
When Agent K asks what
they are singing, they tell her of their
own funeral march. We learn
they are no suspect, and they are no
killer, the unfortunate fragmented
consequences of distraction

Report No. 0058

We all come to a broken line
A or B. Pages torn open or burned
it's amazing what you remember
Agent K inspects their final pictures
side by side, the skeletal remains
of a girl, the decomposed body of
a woman. Both are so similar yet
different, discovered yards from
one another. It must be the same
killer. But what is the message?
Or, should she stop assuming there's
ever a message with murder?
Two dead, years apart, but why?
She begs the universe to unpack for
her. The only thing holding them
together, making them unintended
sisters, are the butterflies that
covered their eyes in agonizing rest
the only motive she can perceive
disintegrates when she wakes to
another day cursed by no answers
palms open praying to nothing
she doesn't crush their delicate wings
Is this what metamorphosis looks like?

Report No. 0059

Asked to submit a report. It reads like this:

Roadkill appeared mysteriously at the place where the skeleton was found, a bouquet of dried roses rested at the base of the tree where our woman was found hanging. Both the dead animal and flowers were wrapped with white ribbon. The carcass, a raccoon, appears to have been struck by a midsize sedan. Tire marks are indistinguishable in the bloodied, tangled fur. Crimson roses appear to have been white, once they smell of fresh spray paint, red for effect later that evening a headless deer drained of blood was discovered at the midpoint of both scenes, a white card was tucked between its left hoof reading in simple black swirling script *Get well soon*

Report No. 0060

Time passes, what we force to hold
still, Agent K continues down long
passageways of her mind, constructs
emptiness, notes names, dates,
it's all settling there, sparkling fibers
like silver tinsel, capturing a flashing
bulb. A line must be sketched. Dreams
are now full of fluttering wings, torn
flesh flapping in the wind, roads slick,
lined with dismembered body parts all
belonging to her. A child stands at the
entrance of the trail wearing a white
paper dress reciting the alphabet backwards
the image pauses and repeats, a VHS tape.
When she wakes, she knows the windows
and doors are open again. She senses this
time she's close.

Report No. 0061

Our corpse is angry
its beauty stripped
taken
deeper down routes
never intended
some thought she
was faking, going
days with her phone
shut off, sought after
silence. Her mother
stutters, dropping
the call, it's a
danger knowing the
only help available
does not include
resurrection, our
woman can rest
we have located
the hiker's family
the funeral is held
analysis stored
now we wait for
the ticking of
postmortem days
to identify our
smallest cadaver
Little Corpse
remaining center
of this mystery

Report No. 0062

Let's speak of theories

The perpetrator was out
creating a shrine for our
Little Corpse. The snap of
twigs nearby signaled a
presence, our woman alone
out for a hike at dusk.
He rises. Our hiker sees
the photo and freshly
collected autumn leaves.
Stones in the outline of a
body. She makes to run
He is faster.
You have crossed a line
You will never cross again
There's rope and struggling
pleading, nothing was seen
of course. He takes
pride in his work, showcasing
destruction with skill
our second victim was
never intended, stumbling
into a moment that led
to her homicide. Our killer
isn't a novice, each movement
is executed with intention
there's always an intermission.
Our third act begins.

Report No 0063

A homicide most
Remote and glorious
Sacrificed to none

Failing to fall silent
As daggers, knives
Bullets, fell, fired

We all dart around
Wondering remains
Capable, culpable

Who among us
Is excited by pain
Squirming violation

There's one here
Within the crowd
Many monsters, you

Report No. 0064

What is the hope? That one day this killer will be caught? Then what? There will be another, springing up between the cracks of cement, deceitful and weaving in through our mornings, parks, bus stops, and parking lots, smiling always a smile that isn't just an innocent expression of benign intent. They look through a mask crafted of practice acting as a human should act, kind, behaving as a person should, trusting, but they've studied our movements like a great actor would memorize monologues and perform soliloquies, this:

"The juxtaposition of memory and change. It makes the experience sharper."

Report No. 0065

Little Corpse's life imagined
Playgrounds and ice cream
Birthday parties, colored balloons

What is a life? A string of milestones
Christmas lights blinking in darkness
Ushering, welcoming endless possibility

What is a life taken, a timeline disrupted?
Kisses that will never brush lover's lips
Hearts that will never fill with purpose

A baby's cries should morph into
an adolescent's giggle, adult laughter
final words spoken should be:
'I love you. I have always loved you'

And not garbled, blood-soaked tears through
Throats tightening, begging, pleading, whimpering:

'Why?'

Report No. 0066

Case closes in, Suspect number 3
there is no record, but there
have been questions, suspicions
Who is this person? No one knows
What was their upbringing like? Their
mother and father, schooling, shall we
profile — a method meant to categorize
label, understand a human's behavior
when actions delve into something
we do not want to detect, deviance,
behavioral characteristics. We must
first analyze the crime:

Victim 1: Jane Doe. Child age 14 to 18
Victim 2: **[INSERT NAME]** age 19 to 25

Victim 1: Killed elsewhere, based on the
decomposition stages of the cadaver.
5 to 10 years ago. Cause of death unknown.

Victim 2: An unplanned killing, likely
stumbled upon killer revisiting crime scene

Victim 1 was moved from covered location
and brought to a wooded area and then
displayed, meaning our killer wanted
their work to be seen, known, admired

But why? Why so many years after the murder? Attention? Boredom? Perhaps they are planning to kill again? What can we determine from a corpse that cannot speak to us? Sing to us? Our suspect sits before us now, confident and curious waiting with eyes that tell Agent K you cannot reconstruct this Modus Operandi

Report No. 0067

To profile with bloodshot eyes
why should we ever presume an
investigator of murders should
be well-rested and in high spirits
optimist and cheerful? Sit
with the ravaged remains of an
infant, a woman shattered, a man
bludgeoned a hundred times,
question if the scent of putrefaction
can ever leave the investigator's
nostrils? Can an investigator ever
silence the screams of a mother
howling lost in agony, in
knowing her only child was
suffocated, raped, mutilated
then decapitated, disemboweled
and stuffed in black garbage
bags, in pieces, scattered across
a city, driven to dump sites, rotting
in trash. Tell me why we should
expect a cheerful investigator?
They're a natural pessimist fully aware
of how hurt is constant, how hurt
reminds them that they're not dead
and they still have a job to do, a job
which exists because of sadistic chaos.
Violence, violation a

nd agony are
our investigator's only guarantee, there
is no faking optimism. Give your investigator
melancholy, trauma. The suffering is
what keeps them moving and alive And our investigators will walk
with this weight, dressed in a
shroud of grief, knowing the depths
of cruelty humans are capable of,
their mind should not wander, but
remain focused and fixed on
screams, the pulse of terror and the
pain of agony, realizing that the killing
will not end when they die, this is
violence in perpetuity so long as
humans live, humans will kill. This
is our investigator's burden
to carry, to step into the lives of victim
and offender, to understand both
innocent and monster. Calculate, profile,
replicate, input data, analyze, evaluate
folding and churning, recreate, trace
movements. Know what it's like to stop
another's breath, know what it's like to
watch eyes flutter into forever sleep
and weep as you listen to confessions
of people who torture and kill, full of
glee with the thrill they watched their
victim beg and convulse beneath their
hands. Why would anyone do this?
There are people out there who do this.

Report No. 0068

Suspect 3 is a person

With a job and a house.
No identifiable markings.
No records. No tickets.
No routines. No priors.

Simple.

Speech is formally informal.
Clothes, hair, and nails are clean.
History? Parents. Siblings. Schooling.
Place of employment is at a location.

There's nothing to set this individual
apart from the others, except for the
unscientific feeling, guess, hunch
that blossoms and blooms within
Agent K that this person knows more

Report No. 0069

Let's make a deduction
There must be a culprit

Playing a less or more
Prominent role, take note

You must concentrate
Searching for clues, patterns

The truth of the problem
Will be apparent if you see

Learn the explanation
Solve the mystery yourself

Does the solution make sense?
Or, should you reread the book?

Ignore long passages, descriptions
Atmospherics holding up action

Is our professional riddled with guilt?
Do we have a thought-provoking crime?

Cause of death should never be
Identified as an accident or suicide

All motive will fall on our investigator
To determine the guilty in this story

Report No. 0070

Our corpse is furious
Agent K can sense
its desiccated throat
tear open and scream
as her own mouth
pulls back with rage,
the tug of sinew
lips parting

You let him leave

Evidence, Agent K
needs "Evidence"
a roadblock that gives
criminals time to flee
escape, and spread
black mold
intuition means nothing
voices alternate, discordant

She touches

Mystery to the solution
forever
detecting, second guessing
pluck my eyes from this
open my chest to feel

what I have determined
there is no denying: this is
our killer

Report No. 0071

The threadbare curtain
lifts, and Little Sister
sees them standing on
the sidewalk. Months
have gone by—or has
it been years?—time is
seasons, school years
new teachers, tests,
it's been a cycle of
summers springs winters
Little Sister remembers
that Autumn so long
ago, the discovery of a
deathly delight, of
beauty in death, her room
now decorated in pinned
pressed butterflies as tribute
the person on the sidewalk
raises a hand and waves
that night she dreams
of wolves, crushed leaves
maggots worming within
exposed fat and blood
crunching succulent bone
a Big Bad Wolf arrives as
promised, they've returned
to blow her house down
dine on her delicate vocal cords
with freshly polished silverware

Report No. 0072

Agent K tells herself
lies, lullabies to sleep
Where did my life go?
it's a spotlight above
a body being dissolved
in a blue vat, blood swirling
puppet strings snapped
human eyes pinned to
soft plastic dolls
she tells herself she's
anxious and cannot
move on, eternally ruined

gripped by a history
of violence repeating
even in tender moments
it's all there, regret and guilt
they will carry her off
her pallbearers are the dead

Report No. 0073

Clues tell us nothing
is warranted or issued
surveillance feeling
unwarranted
the investigation
pivots in directions
fanning outside points
disorganized, useless
Agent K allows their
distraction, honing
in on Suspect 3
remembering the way
through doors and how

tragedy informs her
feelings, our killer
is not retreating, but
planning, weaving
spinning the way
of shallow graves

Report No. 0074

So long as we know, so long as we can say
For you will die, and I will die
Our points meeting at the same destination
What fate is worse than death, I will tell you:
Being murdered by the hands of another

Report No. 0075

Suspicion grows
relentless as our
Suspect 3 spots
Agent K outside

sipping espresso
on a summer's day
café, flipping
through notes
Suspect 3 sighs
"I don't see a
body here," they
whisper under
their breath
and we all live
with a sinking
betrayal that
stands relentlessly
dripping with
significance
Suspect 3 casually
crosses the street
boards a bus, and
Agent K realizes it's
never as she intended
for she has lost
interest in the living
long ago, and for
this crime she will
never falter

Cynthia Pelayo

Report No. 0076

Do you remember me?
Little Sister does not turn
as the car slowly follows
she knows this voice
even though she's never
heard them speak

She remembers many things
about that day, sun, trees
Little Brother whimpering
beautiful bones beneath clear sky
She will not engage, but enters
her home and locks the doors

Outside the parked car waits
Yet, so will she. Upstairs she
turns to her altar of mounted

butterflies, lovely and frozen
vanessa cardui lining her walls
knowing priceless treasure awaits

Report No. 0077

You cannot afford
doubting yourself
wandering in grief
although, it's there
the remembrances
condolences, cards

I'm sorry for your loss

The edges are closing
reflections distorted
true depictions are false
we observe dark lines
knocks on the door
outlasting all hope

Report No. 0078

No supernatural means
No mysterious forces
No mystical elements

Ghosts do not exist
Demons are fairy tales
God is lore

What lives in dark woods
What emerges from depths
What creeps within alleyways

Looks us in the mirror
Clutches our hands
Tells us we're loved

Human as monster
Blaming destruction on
Fables and legends

What's caused the most
Destruction and suffering
A warm beating heart:
It's us

Report No. 0079

Cipher, code
Letter, unravel

Come close,
Locked room

Alibi, proof
The last thing

I say, everything is broken
Under consideration

Lying, beneath
Remarks, a dog barked

Static loose in melody
Floor plan, a knock

What does this mean?

Symmetry, an outline
Disturb, disrupt, desire

Core, unfulfilled
Play your part

Criminal, perpetrator
Nothing is by accident

Report No. 0080

Quiet except
creeping
tip toeing across

wooden floors
At the top of the stairs, it glows

A familiar scent
A familiar noise
Hand over mouth

But this is not how it goes

Report No. 0081

House surrounded
Silent cars
Beating lights against twilight

Pulses thickens with worry
Mistakes if made are paid
In blood, victim or perpetrator

Jackets and bold letters
F.B.I, Fear Before Infinity?
Failed Badges Impact?

Demands to enter, apprehend
A wolf ready to blow
Little Sister's house down

Clues lined up on a map
Dotted with dates, names
Locations, arrows blinking

To our Little Sister no longer
A little girl, a young woman
Sleeping soundly, awakened

Agent K knows it will not end
A murder most performative
Endings begin anew

Report No. 0082

Agent K enters, weapon drawn and eyes active
in the hallway Mother lays dead, strangled with a cord

on the sofa, Father, scissors jutting from his temple
Little Brother, who is no longer a little boy, but a

young man, is slumped at the bottom of the stairs, blood
pooling around him, the wound as of yet, not visible

a single light beckons from the second floor. As Agent K
approaches, she announces her name — Karma
her name the constant reminder that her actions will forever produce a
ripple across the timeline of her life, their lives
once again, she announces her name, and here we hear
the voice of our once Little Sister :

"He's here, but no longer."

Agent K finds our killer on a carpeted floor, neck sliced open, esophagus,
fat, blood and bone exposed, eyes rolled back.

Our once Little Sister sits at the edge of her bed, a knife in hand.

"I've been waiting a long time for him," she says.

Report No. 0083

Years pass, as they should and our Little Corpse remains unidentified, interred with the mournful honor bestowed time again, immemorable, Jane Doe. A great monarch engraved on her headstone. Agent K plants milkweed in her garden, attracting and watching painted ladies fluttering within the reaches of dreams, imagining the possibility or a reality in parallel where our Little Corpse could exist, reborn in brilliance, her fingertips reaching and brushing cautious butterfly wings. Yet Agent K's mind returns to a space occupied and fixed staring into the depths of darkness unreachable by others, for no one should live in a mind like hers, plagued with the knowing of the vicious limits the murderous will take, and of vengeance and revenge that bubbles over into something that cannot be extinguished. Agent K will remain bathed in the dread and guilt of walking with death, unable to hear clearly as specters whisper tragedies through static. The phone will ring again, with another message of another body found, of secrets buried within, and of a great sky above, a galaxy home to stars playing witness to a new tragedy unfold.

Acknowledgements

Thank you forever to Stephanie Wytovich. I forever treasure our friendship, your expertise and skill as an editor and poet, and your guidance.

Thank you to Sara Tantlinger for reading this collection and providing an introduction. I am in awe of your skill and dedication, always.

Thank you to Jennifer Barnes and John Edward Lawson, who are not just my publishers but dear friends. I'm glad to know you and to be able to work with you.

Thank you to Gerardo and my children who hold up all of the pieces and prevent me from coming undone so that I can continue to create.

Finally, thank you to everyone who has read my work, especially *Into the Forest and All the Way Through*, it's because of that collection that *Crime Scene* exists.

Thank you,

Cynthia "Cina" Pelayo

About the Author

Cynthia "Cina" Pelayo is an International Latino Book Award winning and three-time Bram Stoker Awards® nominated poet and author.

She is the author of *Loteria, Santa Muerte, The Missing* and *Poems of My Night*, all of which have been nominated for International Latino Book Awards. *Poems of My Night* was also nominated for an Elgin Award. Her recent collection of poetry, *Into the Forest and All the Way Through* explores true crime, that of the epidemic of missing and murdered women in the United States, and was nominated for a Bram Stoker Award and Elgin Award.

Her modern day horror retelling of the Pied Piper fairy tale, *Children of Chicago* was released by Agora / Polis Books, and won an International Latino Book Award for Best Mystery (2021).

She holds a Bachelor of Arts in Journalism from Columbia College, a Master of Science in Marketing from Roosevelt University, a Master of Fine Arts in Writing from The School of the Art Institute of Chicago, and is a Doctoral Candidate in Business Psychology at The Chicago School of Professional Psychology.

Cina was raised in inner city Chicago, where she still lives.

Find her online at www.cinapelayo.com and on Twitter @cinapelayo.

9 781947 879485